Turtle's Taxi

By Anna Khan

Illustrated by Kirsten Guerin

Target Skill Consonant *Tt*/t/

Scott Foresman
is an imprint of

PEARSON

TODAY'S TURTLE
Trent Hotel
TENANT NOTICE
TRASH
PICK-U
TUESDA
+
THURSDA
10
TOP TURTLE TAXI

turtle

taxi

turkey

telephone

tiger

television

10

ten